CHILD OF SCORN

CHILD OF SCORN:

A Mind Play in Three Parts and Numerous Voices

by

Carol Ann Morizot

Harold House, Publishers
Houston, Texas

Harold House edition, June 1978

ISBN 0-930138-02-3
Library of Congress Catalog Card Number 78-52256

In loving dedication to my parents and the immense contribution that they made to my life.

FOREWORD

This play is designed to utilize to the fullest the more recent aspects of theatrical staging—lighting, close audience involvement, intimacy between performers and audience. Mood, tone, and special effects created by staging and lighting are more essential and critical to the performance than set or properties.

The play, however, is so constructed as to be easily adapted to the conventional stage for a more traditional production. The script is divided into "parts" rather than acts merely to emphasize the relative unimportance of sequential "time" elements in the play. The three parts do correspond roughly to three acts in a more traditional play, except that there is no derivable time relationship essential to understanding the parts individually or collectively. In fact, although the parts cannot be interchanged and retain the meaning and dramatic effect, it is possible the parts could be produced separately for analysis or study. I do not recommend this approach, but I recognize it is a possibility.

The most important link between the parts is the *meaning* relationship which builds through the production promoted by the absorbing effect of the stream of consciousness quality.

NOTE:

To readers and performers of this play—

Please maintain uppermost in your mind and acting that this play is primarily a tone poem about the meaning of death and existence in contemporary society.

Thank you,
C. Morizot

The Players:

Female, preferably Caucasian
Male, preferably Black or Brown

An Adult Chorus consisting of two male and two female voices.

Four children, preferably two male, two female pre-adolescent or early puberty in age range; among the children there should be at least three easily-distinguishable racial types.

Death, a mime

The Crew:

An excellent director
An incredible stage manager
An ambitious lighting and effects director
An intelligent sound effects person
Compassionate stage hands

Playing time: approximately 90 minutes

PART I
The Fall

Setting: *The play begins with a completely darkened stage or arena. The first chorus is spoken by voices placed in the back and on the sides of the audience, or any other arrangement which will from the beginning of the play promote close participation of the audience.*

The first chorus should set the first mood or tone in consciousness through its airy and carnival atmosphere. A totally frivolous sense of anticipation of fun and fantasy barely disguising an underlying current of social ennui should be projected throughout the dialogue.

CHORUS:

Voice 1: October! Yeaaaaay!
Voice 2: Football, Fall, and Fantastic Feelings!
Voice 3: And Halloween!
Voice 4: Weekends in the woods!
Voice 2: On the seashore!
Voice 4: Biking in the country!
Voice 1: Or the city!
Voice 3: Backpacking, popcorn, hot chocolate and buttered rum!
Voice 2: The first snow!
Voice 3: And Halloween!
Voice 4: Things bursting open
Voice 1: Pinatas, pumpkins, and balloons!
Voice 4: Parties and relationships
Voice 2: People bursting with affairs
Voice 3: And Halloween!
Voice 1: Exciting

Choral chant: Hush, Hush, Hush

Voice 1: It is the beginning of winter
All Voices: The last fling, the first crispness, the early snow
Voice 3: And Halloween
Voice 2: Costumes and new fashions
Voice 3: Masks and disguises
Voice 1: Balls and parties
Voice 4: Masquerades and parades
All Voices: Life charges into winter with its own kind of fun,
   but we'll relish October before the play has run!
Voice 2: And the children?
(pause)
All Voices: Counting out their treasures, one by one!

*A tangled cacophony of the voices repeat the next lines by
starting at different places and reading through to the point
where each began.* **Voice 1** *begin at the first sentence.*
Voice 2 *at the third sentence.* **Voice 3** *at the fifth sentence.*
Voice 4 *at the seventh sentence. All voices no matter where
they begin speak the entire paragraph.*

All Voices: Here come the children, Here come the
   questions. Here are the parents. Where are the answers.
   Who are the players. Where are the maskers. What is the
   meaning. Who are the children. Where are they going.
   To parties. To parties. To parties.
   (pause)
Resolution of the voices: Of course!

Scene I: *Immediately after the resolution of the chorus
voices, the lighting reveals (spotlight for best effect) four
children seated cross-legged on the floor center-stage playing One Potato, Two Potato. In the game only two children
at a time are playing (see diagram on next page for
sequence), but all of them are chanting the rhyme:*

One potato, Two potato
Three potato, Four
Five potato, Six potato
Seven potato, More.

The two children playing face each other, one with fists held out in front, the other using a fist to "count" the potatoes. On the hit of Four and More, the child with extended fists withdraws the hit "potato".

As the children proceed with their game, **Death**, *a figure in black leotards with white skeleton and skull mask peers over their shoulders, moving behind each, slowly studying the game and its players like an inquisitive, incredulous observer. The children give no indication of being aware of his presence.*

It is recommended that the children be pre-adolescent or in early puberty with at least three separate and easily distinguishable racial types.

The children play the game chanting and laughing appropriately. The cycling of partners continues until **Death** *slowly settles back on his heels having watched the game from every angle and perspective available to the setting. The pitch of the laughter increases through the scene in volume and intensity.*

1.   Child 1 ⟩⟨ Child 2

       Child 3 ⟩⟨ Child 4

2.   Child 1   Child 2
           ✕   ✕
       Child 3   Child 4

3.   Child 1 ＼ ／ Child 2
                   ✕
       Child 3 ／ ＼ Child 4

Scene II: *As the spotlight dims on the children who continue the pantomime of the game, another spotlight comes up on a couple for the next scene.*

Setting: *A black man is standing with one foot propped on a chair next to a very antique, but pristine table at which a white woman is seated. Each has some sort of personal "business" to give the impression of preoccupation (but please, actors and players, no newspapers for the man or kitchen apron for the woman. The player should feel comfortable with the business and it should be something progressive and yet innocuous such as cutting out strings of paper dolls, stringing beads, tying knots in rope, making beer-tab jewelry or daisy-chain necklaces, etc.) The whole impression should convey a non-productive routine.*

Female:
    I feel cold.
Male:
    It's winter.
    I feel it too
    crawling out of the night
    with its cold feet treading
    on our hearts but

    we won't notice it so much if
    we keep busy.
Female:
    Yes, busy. I have
    more to do today than ten humans

    my life just can't hold all of these
    (she holds up whatever she is doing)
    what are you doing? *(he shows her)*

    can we go to sleep earlier than usual this evening?

Male:
>I think we ought to
>with the children being
>entertained all day and then
>the partying all afternoon.
>
>we'll all begin to notice winter
>coming on, the healthy shadows and our own
>figures collecting caricature

Female:
>From the weather?

Male:
>Yes, and the children
>
>winter will close them in
>robbing us of the freedom that the
>summer has imposed
>
>the house will swell like a
>bubble on a hose from the wealth
>of their confusion

Female: *(sarcastically)*
>Diffusion, you mean.
>
>All over the house they will
>interrupt my logical work of grief

Male:
>Your imposition.

Female: *(obviously ignoring his comment)*
>I doubt that I will find
>the strength or means to
>bear their force
>I don't think I'll survive
>my own desire for freedom
>hanging on the vines of their
>cruel containment

I am afraid I shall be
changing more than they are.

Male:
Yes, we are both changing,
the world closes in upon us
with this winter approaching

we can only trust our wits and wisdom
to be shifting like the winds;
our heads, bending daily to the
lowered slant of light.

Female:
And earlier and earlier everyday
we'll go to bed

Male:
But still accomplish more and more
each day.

Female:
At least, you will in your world
leaving the house early and returning late,
but I am isolated by the weather, the objections,
and the fears

I always seem to find myself at odds
with hours and the children and the
antiquated voices of our parents
telling over and over what they
thought was right.

I will be frigid when you want me and
torrid when you're out. I will be helpless.

I will love the children but will not
know how to touch them fearing I will ruin
their innocence. I will be happy when they
are at school. They will be happy too.

For no apparent reason the male and female act out a ritual of swapping places, changing chairs around as if rearranging the setting, and from under the table finding in a box masks which they exchange. They change places while putting on the mask of opposite sexuality/color. The lighting has come up and is now very bright, yellowish, harsh.

Female mask:
>Now I am here tied to the weather and
>the fears and I am struggling against the
>odd hours and the contained enthusiasm of
>the children.
>
>I will envy them when they go to school.
>I will love them but I know I will resent
>their leaving home and coming back to me
>with their arms fuller than their minds,
>their hearts higher than their knees.
>
>I will be lonely.
>They will be needy.

Male mask:
>We will be close though.
>I will help you and when these words
>stretch out across the empty spaces,
>we will feel deep tingles in our spines.

Female mask:
>Will you love me?

Male mask:
>Whatever that means.
>Yes. I promise I will help.

Female mask:
>I am afraid of you.
>Our love may be our illness.

Male mask: *(sternly)*
>Don't make me worry that our needs
>form only 'crevices to catch despair.

It cannot happen yet
Female mask: *(interrupting)*
when we are trying.
Male mask:
Yes. When we accept our separate sicknesses
until together we form health.
Female mask:
Are we abusing it?
Male mask:
No, only assessing it.
Female mask:
For how long?
Male mask:
For as long as it takes.

Lights out on the set.

Scene III: *A warm, rosy lighting comes up slowly on the set which holds two rows of primitive wooden chairs. There are three chairs on each side with an "aisle" down the middle. The children's voices are heard off-stage or in the back of the audience playing hide-and-go-seek.*

Voice 1:
1, 2, 3, 4, 5, 6, 7, 8, 9, 10
Ready or not
Here I come!
Voice 2:
Can't find me!
Voice 3:
I hear the school bus coming!
Voice 4:
Ollie, ollie, eee
All that's out can come in free!

The children run onstage carrying books, wearing jackets, hats indicating cold weather. They take their places in the chairs as if getting onto a crowded school bus. During the following scene they act as though they are riding to school, gazing out of the windows and obviously interacting with each other under the monitoring eye of an adult who allows few deviations from the rules. Discipline and rigidity are key responses in this and the classroom segment which follows.

Child 1:
I feel myself beginning today.
I may be important by tonight;
I may be seen as human by this afternoon.
Tomorrow there are those who'll say I'm civilized.
Then I know I'll be important, but
will I still be me?

Child 2:
Do you want to be important or free?

Child 3:
Free or ridiculous?

Child 4:
Ridiculous or dead

Child 1: *(giggling)*
Dead, of course.

Children laugh.

Child 1: *(pensively)*
Isn't death the middle of all things;
isn't being dead being free?
(turning to the child next to him)
Don't you remember me?

Child 2: *(surprised)*
Remember what?

Child 4:
Yes, tell us what exactly
that thought
is supposed to mean.

Child 3:
Yes, what should we remember?

Child 1:
Not should, but may
Remember who you used to be.

Child 2: *(looking down at hands and body)*
>This person that I am is
>all I have of me.

Child 4:
>If now is the figment of the mind,
>I think I know
>what you may mean.
>I think I understand.

Child 3:
>I don't think I can, but
>I think I want to learn.
>Who do you think you ought to be?

Child 1:
>All I mean to say is that the simple
>world of what we are becoming is
>the deadly magic of learning *how* to be,
>but the art and science of it is
>peculiarly simple and inexpressibly free

Child 2:
>I love magic.

Child 3:
>There's a magic show at school today.

Child 4:
>Of course there is, and
>here we are now among the others
>in the auditorium.

Child 1:
>And the show is free!

Death *enters as the magician in a top hat. The children applaud him, and he proceeds with tricks and sleights of hand in a game of pretense in which they participate wholeheartedly with visible and audible expressions of amazement.*

Child 2:
>Here is the enchanting magician
>sent by the parents to entertain us.

Child 3:
    His figure should be frightening
    only if his face seems unfamiliar,
    but it doesn't.

Child 4:
    Watch how he deceives us so
    perceptively! What a strange vocation!

Child 1:
    But he does it with those mirrors;
    can't you see?

Child 4:
    Yes, I see he does it with the mirrors
    and with the power of suggestion, he
    creates each new illusion.
    And he thinks we shall continue to believe.

Child 2:
    And I shall for one believe him
    As long as he can keep me entertained.

Child 3:
    I only want to know how does he do it?
    The hand faster than my eyes and the hat
    filled to the brim with the cankers of a
    million diseases.

Child 2: *(as if hypnotized)*
    Fascinating, isn't he?
    A kaleidescope of tragedies *(clapping hands)*.

Child 4:
    Wars, plagues, and a million indiscretions
    pulled from the pockets of his frock coat
    just like the tricks and treats that flood
    our minds from a lifetime of TV.

Child 3:
    But I love it and after all,
    it's free!

Child 1: *(smiling)*
    And I must admit
    it *is* entertaining. Fascinating

if you choose the various viewpoints and
quickly change your thinking to reflect
ghosts, or rapists, or identify with
mass annihilations of entire societies.
It can be fun! And after all,
it's only sham, a fleshy pool of
make-believe.

Child 4: *(squinting)*
How can he keep us from seeing what
he's doing?

Child 2:
He's keeping our attention.

Child 3:
Yes, I cannot take my eyes off of him.

Child 4:
And the hands are quick.

Child 1:
Faster than we think,
he works his magic on us.
He charms us with his act
and builds our confidence in him
by small degrees.

Child 2:
He works his magic on us.

Child 3:
And on our parents.

Child 4:
But they do not seem to see him.
At least they do not seem to see
the way they make he seem to you and me.

Child 1:
They cannot cope with his illusions.
They find his bag of tricks upsetting.

Child 4:
They watch with us and then pretend
they never knew him. What do children know
that they cannot accept?

Child 1: *(quietly, nodding his head with eyes downcast)*
>The truth,
>Perhaps.
>Perhaps the truth.

Lights out suddenly.

Scene IV: *As the spotlight comes up, the male is seated crosslegged on the floor taking apart an engine. The female is behind the table which is filled with cooking paraphernalia. She is dropping cookies one by one onto a cookie sheet in the center of the table. Both have the masks of opposite sexuality dangling from ropes around their necks. They appear to have aged considerably since the first scene in which they appeared* **(Scene II).**

Female:
>Noon already and I haven't done enough
>to justify having lived so many years.

Male:
>You will though.
>There is still time for what you need.
>It won't be much longer until you see . . .

Female: *(interrupting sarcastically)*
>A panacea for our mutual disease?

Male:
>Even for that there may still be time
>if you believe . . .

Female: *(interrupting again)*
>I think I am confusing it,
>one thing leads to another like a string of
>worry beads and I wonder if I understand
>anything at all about this place or who
>you are or who I am or why we thought
>we knew the meaning of existence when we
>learned the power of our genitals and the
>innocent ability we had to breed and breed and breed
>and Breed!

Male: *(walks over and puts his arms around her comforting her)*
  You are confusing it, but I am listening.
  I hear your sorrow sleeping beside me in the
  dark and I grieve for you and I would
  help you if I could.
Female: *(returning to her cooking)*
  You *can* help. You are here where I am.
  You are listening and you are after all
  different, but like me.
  We are the same species.
  We are anthropos.
  We are erectus.
  We are Homo sapiens just like these
  children who toy with us.
Male: *(picking up some item from the table)*
  What are you making?
Female:
  Swamp-ghost pastries, fly pies, weed-mush
  sandwiches, and pickled bat's blood punch,
  to mention only the most essential ingredients
  on the list.
Male: *(returning to his work)*
  I only hope the children know how much to
  eat of each. I hope they don't get sick.

  I watch them in the mornings,
  small, delicate things extending their
  weak grasp through their play.
  Unlike our progressively more arthritic fingers
  their young hands fold and unclose easily.

  Their joyous behavior reminds me of the bees
  we used to keep. In summer they flitted
  carelessly from flower to flower under
  the grandiose charms of the heavy trees.
  I look at the children and think
  they know something we must have forgotten

about the meaning of existence.
Female: *(interrupting her own work to look at him)*
    But I am only one of their flowers.
    I will be dead before they realize how
    they needed me, before they learn to
    appreciate the way they used me, drained me, poured
    me into their frame, pulled my wealth
    and beauty into the fame and fortune they
    desired.

    Like petals, all my feelings are dying
    one by one
    and soon the best of me will lie beneath
    the snow until whatever comes.

A bell rings and the masks go on and while the lights dim slightly, the male and female change places.

Female mask:
    Now I am the one who will know something
    before the snow completely blanks me out;
    I shall be ready.
    I will learn the answer to the puzzle
    before it blanks me out.
Male mask:
    I admire your courage.
    You manage everything so well. Even your smells
    and secret nooks are like Halloween.
    Persuasive.
Female mask:
    But I hear the excitement building in other
    regions.
Male mask:
    I hear your clock on the stair and it
    is distinctly irritating?
Female mask:
    Like a mask that doesn't fit?

Male mask:
>Yes, and like the noise of the striking arm
>which does not quite clear the bells and
>drags us past with it every new hour, gaining
>momentum. As reliable and aggravating as
>the ocean.

Female mask:
>And as never-ending as the variegated tide. *(pause)*
>What worries me most is the mirror
>standing as it does in the bathroom.
>It has the best position from which to
>wink and stare at my dwindling perfection.

Male mask: *(startled)*
>Nothing about you has changed.

Female mask:
>Maybe my weight is the same, but an
>older person not totally unfamiliar blocks
>the threshhold now with a somewhat thicker
>frame. And I see possibilities there which
>may be harboring a million intricate diseases
>caused by aging.
>
>A dull knife is carving back my muscle
>and limiting my power. And I have lost
>all hope of staying even, much less
>winning.

Male mask: *(takes the partner in his arms and begins to
make an awkward waltz around the room; music fades
in (a technically fine Chopin or Strauss waltz, but one
which is fairly unfamiliar); the music picks up and their
movements improve until they are gliding gracefully
across the floor, then they dance faster and faster. The
masks come off, but they continue dancing until they
fall on the floor in exhaustion)*
pause.
>*(still breathing hard and laughing)*
>We shall dance away the curse of all our kind

and they shall learn from us the craft of dying!
Lights out.

*A spotlight comes up at the opposite side of the play area
and the costumed* **Death** *walks into the widening spot. The
children follow him, Pied-Piper style. He circles the stage
area and returns to sit cross-legged in the spotlight opposite
the couple who remain immobile. The children grab hands
and circle around* **Death** *singing:*

Children:
    Here we go round the mulberry bush,
    The mulberry bush, the mulberry bush;
    Here we go round the mulberry bush,
    So early in the morning, so early in the
    morning.

    Here we go round the mulberry bush,
    The mulberry bush, the mulberry bush;
    Here we go round the mulberry bush,
    As if it were a tree, as if it were a
    tree.

Lights out.

A very brief intermission.

PART II
The Trip

Scene I: *Two rows of two chairs each simulating an automobile are set on one side of the stage under lights. The* **Female** *enters dressed in dark, but not black clothing, a suit or slacks set which would be appropriate for a fall football game.*

Female: *(calling over her shoulder)*
>   Don't forget to lock the back door
>   from the inside. Mother has the key to the
>   front door if she needs anything.

(pauses and half turns as if listening to a voice she can hear, but the audience cannot)
>   O.K., but I set the timers for the lamps.
>   Just leave the bathroom light on.
>   And the one on the back porch, too.

(She turns and gets into the car—the chairs—from the passenger side as the car is set diagonally in the set. She is loaded down with a thermos, blankets, purse, and a huge paper sack. She arranges the items around her and then sits for a few seconds, looks at watch, and begins to fidget impatiently).

Death *enters (costumed as before) pauses and stares searchingly around the audience. With an apparent air of nonchalance and diffidence, he exits and then returns carrying a stadium blanket over his arm. He gets into the back seat of the "car" and settles in much as the* **Female** *did as if preparing for a long ride.*

Female: *(checking her watch again and then looking off
    stage)*
    What
    are you doing? We're late if we don't
    start now. You know I hate to miss the
    pre-game activities *(mumbling to herself)*
    and *you* hate to miss the kick-off!
    (strains as if listening to an unheard response)
    Do you want me to come do it?
    (obviously frustrated by the reply, the **Female** *does no*
    get out of the car, but begins fussing with the para
    phernalia around her—any personal business which
    suggests impatience, irritation, etc.)
Male: *(appears wearing bright, sporty clothing, carrying*
    keys, a map stuck under his arm)
    I had to find the keys, Babe. I'm so used to hiding things
    from burglars that I can't keep up with anything myself
    anymore.
    (he is as oblivious to the **Female's** *annoyance as to the*
    presence of **Death** *in the back seat)*
    Would you look up the turns while I get this thing on the
    road?
    (he hands her the map)
Female: *(studying the map while he makes turning gestures*
    with the illusory wheel and then continues to simulate
    driving; **Death** *folds his arms across his chest and yawns in a*
    sleepy, bored manner)
    First, we want to turn left on I-30 and it looks like that
    will take us to . . .
Male: *(interrupting)*
    One thing at a time, please.
    Just don't go to sleep on me.
    I don't want to waste time stopping to
    look at the map like last time.
Female: *(sarcastically)*
    Or wind up getting lost and wandering in
    the wilderness for forty days and forty nights.
    Have you got the tickets?

Male: *(patting chest pocket)*
 Sure, right here near my heart!
 What time is it now?
Female: *(looking at watch)*
 About four. We should have almost an
 hour to get something to eat
 before the pre-game show.
Male:
 Fantastic! I'm starved already.
 Have you got the coffee handy?
Female: *(fumbles around and opens the thermos and pours
 coffee into the lid)*
 Sure.

Death *sighs heavily, looks at watch, yawns again and then
settles back as if to take a nap.
The couple continue to ride; the* **Female** *finds another cup
and pours herself coffee, then she mimes watching the
scenery while the* **Male** *juggles coffee and drives. The lights
begin to change colors simulating the setting sun as the*
Chorus *speaks this next section. As in the first part, the
chorus voices are arranged in the audience. As the* **Chorus**
ends, the stage goes dark on the "car" and its passengers.

CHORUS:

Voice 1:
 Is this the way her world ends
 Not with a bang, but a whimper?
Voice 2:
 Eliot's world did.
Voice 3:
 But is this Eliot's world? Is *she* part of Eliot's
 world? Do human voices wake *her?*
Voice 4:
 No. Not yet.
 There are no voices yet, human or otherwise.

Only the humming of the tires on her own wax
in her own ears.
All the voices, whispered and strained:
No voices reach her; no voices and
No sound.

Voice 4:
Only the purring of the roulette tires.

Voice 1:
Only the murmur of the ice growing on the trees
and the chilly silent patterns of her thoughts
throwing shadows on the ground.

Voice 3:
Longer, colder shadows than the irritating sweat
she collects in the palm of one hand.

Voice 2:
Or the prickly sensation of her cramped feet
going to sleep in their boots from the cold.

Voice 1:
Before she wakes to drown.

Voice 4:
Yes, before she knows she actually exists
pasted though she is against such solid background,
head and shoulders touching nothing but the
cardboard of her limited dreaming.

Voice 3:
Will we announce when the time is nearing?
Will we help them to be ready?

Voice 2:
We, who hear and see, and remember nothing?

Voice 1:
We, who see what it is necessary to forget?

Voice 4:
We, who wink and out pops disaster?

Voice 1:
We, who breathe them comfort at the last
when living is reduced to atoms which are
frozen with the dust?

All the voices speak in hushed tones in a fugue motif, each starting at the beginning stanza after the **Voice** *preceding has reached the second stanza.*

> Winter is coming
> our innocence freezes.
>
> Winter is coming
> to discharge diseases.
>
> Winter is coming
> to turn our lives black.
>
> Winter is coming
> stretched out like a desert.
>
> Winter is coming
> to blow our minds back!

Lights out.

Spotlight comes up on the four children who have taken their places in the dark on the opposite site of the stage from the "car" during the chorus fugue. They are seated on sleeping bags playing "Old Maid" cards in their pajamas. As they continue playing, the lights come up slightly on the "car" revealing the **Female** *asleep against the "window", and the* **Male** *almost hunched over the wheel with a beer in his hand.* **Death** *wakes up, stretches, and then leans between the couple looking at the children opposite.*

Child 1:
> I'm out! I won! I won!

Child 2:
> Let's play again.

Child 3:
> No, I'm sleepy and sick and
> I'm lonely.

Other children: *(amazed)*
Lonely?
Child 3: *(staring blankly around the audience)*
Halloween isn't over yet, is it?
Child 4: *(humming and picking up the cards)*
Well, yes and no. I'm not sure what
time it is. *(looks at 3)*
What are you looking for?
Child 3:
The Photographer.
Child 2: *(incredulously)*
The what?
Child 3: *(trance-like)*
That slow and deadly power which
claims an image with its hard black breath;
that same poor power which resting in a
man's hand needs only to be developed.
(the other children look at each other in a worried fashion)
Child 1: *(shrugs and turns to 3)*
Are you seeing something?
Child 2:
Yes, are you all right? is there something
we are missing? A person taking our photographs
through the night? Taking our pictures?
Child 4:
Halloween is the evening when souls
return to plague us with forgetting
they are dead. That must be the reason
we feel strange; that is why *(looking at 3)*
you think we are under observation.
Child 1:
It's all a matter of what you believe in.
Child 2:
Or what you want that you cannot share.
Child 4:
Or accepting knowledge that you know you shouldn't
have.

Child 3: *(stands up and stares out at the audience)*
    Or having the knowledge of certain things
    you do not want to know.
All the children form a circle with clasped hands around
Child 3 *and repeat with eyes closed tightly:*
    These are the ghosts that haunt us.
    Here is the carcass.
    Pretending is the only game the
    world expects us to play.
They open their eyes and drop their hands somewhat
relieved.
Child 1:
    It is deceiving.
Child 2:
    It is because we are so perceptive.
Child 3: *(half-smiling and holding his stomach)*
    and nauseated.
Child 4:
    and not always happy.

Lights out immediately.

CHORUS: *(with stage completely dark)*
Voice 1:
    The end is coming.
Voice 2:
    The end or the beginning?
Voice 1:
    The end. Just that.
    Simply the end.
Voice 2:
    The beginning must come later.
Voice 3:
    After the contest of the end.
Voice 4:
    We will not watch it.
Voice 2:
    We will not imagine it.

Voice 3:
> We will ignore the part it plays
> in what we call existence.

Voice 1:
> We will say it has no meaning,
> no personal significance.

Voice 2:
> We will believe it is senseless,
> void like a baby's mouth, innocent, maybe,
> but just as toothless.

Voice 4:
> We will keep it from each other for
> as long as we can until we're forced by
> circumstance to face it.

Voice 3:
> Then after brief and shocking glimpses
> we'll erase it.

Voice 4:
> That will make it go away.

Voice 1:
> Of course. Away from us
> and away from the children.

Voice 2:
> And that will be the end of it.

Voice 3:
> Yes. The end certainly.

Voice 4:
> Convenient, politic and rational.
> But not a subject for discussion.

All the voices together very succinctly:
> Of course not.

There is a slight pause, then the chorus members leap from their seats while an enormous crash is heard, sirens go off, voices scream and a general confusion is created on the stage area. The chairs of the "car" are overturned to simulate a car wreck, belongings scattered. The **Female** *is lying with a chair across her abdomen, pinned in the*

*wreckage. Strobe lights flash to give the impression of
ambulances and police cars arriving. As the lights come up
slightly, two chorus members are carrying the* **Male** *off.
Noise continues while the chorus members return and begin
to attend to the business of consulting with witnesses,
picking up the scattered debris, etc.*

Death *enters wearing a white lab coat over his costume
with a stethoscope in hand, bends over the* **Female** *and
begins a routine check of her vital signs. The chorus
members who carried off the* **Male** *have returned and
struggle to lift the chair off the* **Female**, *but their attempts
are unsuccessful. They withdraw to one side and have an
avid discussion obviously about how to lift the wreckage.
Mime is very important to convey the emotional feeling of
the automobile wreck and its aftermath.*

*The sounds diminish and an amber light settles around
the* **Female** *and her medical attendant,* **Death.**

Female: *(traumatized, weak, zombie-like from the shock)*
    I am lying here pinned between this wreckage
    and some final conclusion,
    between chaos and the mist.

    There is nothing left to do except
    review the situation;
    even these thoughts have a life of their own
    now

    Fading slowly to the tune of my confusion.
    What are we doing *(stares up into the face of* **Death***)?*
    Please don't look away or try to think of
    something that will be amusing.

    Am I dying? **(Death** *nods affirmatively)*

    This is it then, this the last of
    what I have been waiting for,
    the final clause in the paragraph,

the final chance for resoluteness,
the last act of my personal play,

the death of my physical being.

How strange there is no grief involved,
no fear, no inhibitions.
Lying here in this crushed flesh
for the first time in my life
I know I'm human.

Female *tries to move, but realizing she is paralyzed, relaxes.* **Death** *bends over and takes the upper body cradling it in his arms with such comforting business as wiping her face, smoothing her hair; he pulls the* **Female** *to a half-reclining position and as he does the chair falls off.*

Female: *(looks up, smiling into* **Death's** *face)*
Thank you, old friend; now I remember you.
(looking around at the audience blankly)
It isn't life now I see from this position
parading before me it's dreams and indecisions,
or all those violet ambitions.
I have no choices left;
not anymore.
(she looks down toward her feet, straining through a momentary panic)

All the old lights are blinking out
One by one;
finite powers carry such sublime
justice, such avarice, such greed

And in the end all we are is pushed
from the wrapping of this clay shell—

So terrifying an experience we couldn't
speak about it at the thought of being

dragged before our time through Hell.

But now I analyze it:
I feel cells, blood vessels curling up in my toes.
A swarm of sensation is fading from my legs.
My heart has stopped, gone out, the blood
settling in my veins like split rails.

No more does centrifugal force spin it
toward my brain. In just eight minutes now
my mind will be stomped out—dreams,
memory, all the world's most friendly delusions.

There is nothing I would covet now to
stop the flood or change this backward motion.
Until the tide is in, it can't go out
and I was never anything but a container.

Death *lays down the head and arranges the body slowly for the funeral, placing hands across the waist and straightening what remains to be straightened about the set. Then he stands at the head of the corpse, folding his hands like a priest after taking vestments from his pockets and draping them over his smock.*

Scene II: *The funeral. While the "priest" continues to stand over the body, flowers are brought and placed in stands at each end; very softly at first, Bach's* Toccata and Fugue in D Minor *is heard in the background. The chorus files by, looks at the body and then stands back to wait for the service to begin.*

Voice 1:
She looks so life-like.
Voice 2:
Hardly bruised.
Voice 3:
She looks as if she could be breathing.
Voice 4:
Or about to move.
Voice 2:
She's still so beautiful. I think her lips seem almost ready to create a smile.
Voice 3:
She is a vision.
Voice 1:
She was a child.

Pause while the music comes up slightly in the background and the priest lifts his hands to signify that the service is about to begin. The next lines are delivered in loud stage whispers as if during the actual service while the "priest" continues a mumbled oratory over the body. The chorus members stand in rows, two on each side of an imaginary isle facing the catafalque in front of the minister.

Voice 2:
She would have been crippled, you know.
Voice 3:
Or worse. She could have been a vegetable.
Voice 1:
Such a pity. Even if she had lived, her life would have been wasted.

Voice 4:
>It's a blessing that she died.
>God's blessing in dusguise.

Voice 1.:
>They say *he* had been drinking.

Voice 4: *(gasping)*
>No!
>*(1 responds by shaking head)*

Voice 2:
>She would have wanted it this way.
>Not a burden to anyone, least of all,
>her family.

Voice 4: *(choking up)*
>Yes, it's true. We are the ones who are unhappy.

The priest completes his ritual and comes to place his arm on each member of the chorus in a gesture of sympathy. Then he stands back almost out of the lighted stage area.

The chorus resumes its liturgy, crying into sleeves and handkerchiefs while the music still plays softly in the background.

CHORUS:
>We are the ones who suffer.

(pause)
>We and the little ones entrusted to us.

(pause)
>We must remember our sister.

(pause)
>We are the ones who are suffering.

(pause)
>Peace, sister, rest.

(pause)
>We are the people who hurt.

(pause)
>Peace, sister, rest.

(pause)

(through clenched teeth)
We are the jackals who hate her, hate her, hate her.
(pause)
Peace, sister, rest.
(pause)
We are the vermin who steal what she
leaves us and devour her flesh.
(pause)
Peace, rest.

The **Chorus** *members begin to take up imaginary stones
from the ground and throw them on the grave in mime. The
music tempo increases and swells under the intensity of the
next section of chorus. Emotions are visibly rampant on the
faces of the mourners.* **Death** *slips out of the scene entirely.*

Voice 1:
Why did you do this?
Voice 2:
How could you treat us like this?
Voice 3:
You monster-bitch!
Voice 4:
You incredible demon!
Voice 2:
You always hated it here.
You wanted to die; even if you never
said it, you secretly wished it. Didn't you?
(the other voices echo in an accusatory round)
Voice 4:
Didn't you?
Voice 2:
Didn't you?
Voice 3:
Didn't you!
Voice 1:
Didn't you?

Now like a pack of wolves they circle the "grave" chanting in unison: Didn't you, didn't you, didn't you, didn't you, etc.

After one full circle, they stop and stare at the body again.

Voice 2:
Why don't you answer us, you fucking whore!
Slut! Hell's angel!

Voice 3: *(kicking at the body)*
She's worthless to us now.
We won't speak evil of the dead.

Voice 4:
If we could tear her limb from limb,
pull out her heart and eyes and eat them,
and pick the marrow from her bones,
she would not answer.

Music stops abruptly.

CHORUS: *(in unison)*
There is no avoiding what has happened.
There is no denying it.
There is no use trying to remember her.
She is dead.
Fuck it!
She is dead.

(pause)

Voice 1: *(turning to leave)*
Let's forget about it.

Voice 2:
That's all over. Let's go get a drink.

Voice 3:
How about a game of pool or a football game on television?

Voice 4:
Hey, great! Beer and backgammon. My throat is parched from swallowing that liturgy.

All turn to leave and move with arms around each other in a common expression of camaraderie. As they reach the other

side of the lighted stage area, **Voice 1** *holds up a hand and
stops to face the group:*
>Only one more thing.
>Don't forget.
>Not a word to the children.
>Their mother is in heaven.

Lights out suddenly.

Intermission

PART III
The Party

Scene I: *The* **Male** *enters carrying his mask of opposite sexuality. Pots of flowers sit on chairs, the floor, the same pristine table is in the center of the stage covered with pots of wilted and half-dead flowers (no fresh flowers, but some straw, plastic, and "used" arrangements preferable). Lighting in soft tones of blues and greens spot the stage. The* **Male** *crosses slowly to the chair next to the table where he was standing in the opening scene of* **PART I.** *He absently removes the pots of dying flowers in the chair and sits staring around the audience in a mood of abject despair. Unconsciously, he is toying with the mask, the rope dangling toward the floor. The* **Female's** *mask is lying on the floor in front of the table; he notices it, but makes no move to retrieve it.*

During the **Chorus,** *he sits quietly as though the spoken words were his thoughts trying to come to grips with life catching on brief scraps of poetry to ease his suffering. Anything the actor can do here in the way of personal tension to augment the emotion of the scene is recommended, but caution should be used in over-dramatizing and virtuosity. At all times the involvement of the audience is critical and crucial to the creation of the play.*

The **Chorus** *as in the other scenes is seated in the audience or if traditional theatre setting is used, around the sides of the auditorium.*

CHORUS: *(in unison in a stage whisper)*
The poets speak to the man. The poets speak.
Softly, quietly, softly.
Let them speak.

Voice 1:

I am Stephen Crane:
"In the desert
I saw a creature, naked, bestial.
Who, squatting upon the ground,
Held his heart in his hands,
and ate of it.

"I said, 'Is it good, my friend?'
'It is bitter—bitter,' he answered;
'But I like it
Because it is bitter,
And because it is my heart.'

Voice 1: *(continuing)*

"I cried, 'Well, but—
The sand, the heat, the vacant horizon.'
A voice said, 'It is no desert.' "

(—Stephen Crane, "In the Desert")

Voice 2:

Robinson's "Miniver Cheevy, child of scorn,
Grew lean while he assailed the seasons;
He wept that he was ever born,
And he had reasons."

(—Edward Arlington Robinson, "Miniver Cheevy")

Voice 3:

Wasn't it Eliot who prophesied:
"This is the way the world ends;
This is the way the world ends;
This is the way the world ends,

Voice 4:

Not with a bang—

Voice 1:

But a whimper."

(—T.S. Eliot, "The Hollow Men")

*Pause while the **Male** reaches under the table and pulls out a bottle of liquor and a glass and pours himself a drink. He bolts down one or two glasses full, then raises a mock toast,*

*drinks it down, and throws the glass so that it breaks against
a large pot of flowers.*

Voice 4:
"Dust thou art, to dust thou shall return!"

CHORUS: *(in unison while the* **Male** *rises and puts on his
mask of opposite sexuality, then wanders over to sit on the
edge of the table)*
Hush, hush, hush
The man is thinking.
Hush, hush, hush,
The man is dying
Hush, hush, hush
  The man will awaken on his own.
  Quietly now. Softly. Listening to the sounds
  of his spirit shaking.

Voice 2:
Virginia Woolf was a modern person. She understood.
Her words still hang like prophecy in the air:

Voice 3:
"Some people go to priests; others to poetry; I to
my friends, I to my own heart, I to seek among phrases
and fragments something unbroken—I to whom there is
not beauty enough in moon or tree; to whom the touch
of one person with another is all, yet who cannot grasp
even that, who am so imperfect, so weak, so unspeak-
ably lonely. There I sat."

(—Virginia Woolf, THE WAVES)

(pause.)

Voices 1 and 4: *(alternating lines)*
Marianne Moore.
"The world's an orphans' home.
Shall we never have peace without sorrow?
without pleas of the dying for help that won't come?
O quiet form upon the dust, I cannot look and yet
I must.

If these great patient dyings—all these agonies—
and woundbearings and bloodshed—
can teach us how to live, these dyings were not wasted."

(Marianne Moore, "In Distrust of Merits")

(pause)

The **Male** *still wearing his mask walks behind the table and
begins to throw dead flowers into the large kitchen trash can
nearby. After a few minutes, he sits down staring at a dead
flower in his hands.*
  The **Chorus** *begins chanting in unison: (softly)*
   *Judas Goat, Judas Goat, Judas Goat, Judas Goat,
Judas Goat, Judas Goat, Judas Goat . . .*

  The **Male** *throws the dead flower he's been fingering on
the floor to lie among the pieces of broken glass while the*
Chorus *continues to chant. He gets up, kicks at the glass in
anger, sees the* **Female's** *mask again, squats down and
picks it up. Sitting on the floor, he removes his own mask and
replaces it with the* **Female's** *mask. Now he is a male
wearing a male mask. At the end of this last chorus selection,
he takes both masks and throws them as hard as he can, then
the lights go out immediately.*

CHORUS: *(in a stage whisper)*
 Judas Goat!
Voice 2:
  "I am ready to let everything around me die/
  the flowers
  aching in the sunlight
  will go first
  and then the garden I have tended for so long
  will be strangled/
  the savage weeds taking hold and seeing my
  indifference will
  never let go

Voice 4:
    . . . the animals will not suffer long/
    one by one
    I will snuff them out like candles,

    no blood spilled/
    no prayers unanswered
    only a few mortal cries
    before the end

Voice 3: *(the* **Male** *wearing the male mask begins looking around the set)*
    but the house will be last/
    I will close the shutters and
    tie up the doors/
    the dead paint will tell its lies
    to the hours
    erasing eons of arrogant care
    and finally my footsteps on the staircase
    will evaporate,
    the silence starving the hallways and bedrooms

Voices 1 & 4:
    there will be nothing to remind others
    of what once existed/
    there will be peace and the enormous
    gift of an absence of pain,

Voices 2 & 3:
    something new growing out of the past
    innocently like wild roses/
    there will be something worthwhile then

Voice 1:
    in my place/

Voice 4:
    the black tunnels of the night will be

relinquished for the elements/
the earth and its gravity
will rearrange my face/
I will stop crawling and unbend
straightened by the force of that
pure annihilation/

All the Voices:
life will be over

(pause)

Voice 2:
and you will be wherever you are now
and I'll never know why
you had to leave me

(—Carol Ann Morizot, "Judas Goat")

Lights out immediately.

Scene II: *The Halloween Party at last! The children enter carrying brightly-colored streamers, jack-o-lanterns, balloons, noise-makers, etc. They are costumed as a robot, a witch, a gypsy, and a pirate. Using tape they begin to decorate the chairs, moving the dead flowers and arrangements to one side of the staging area. Two of the children sweep up the glass, etc. The other two spread the table with goodies.*

Witch: *(singing in a loud, but not very melodious voice)*
    Oh, I'm the wicked witch of the west
    I've come to fetch you as my guest
    And I'll take you wherever you choose,
    If I want to. If I want to.

    I can whip us some chocolate eggs
    That will make you wiggle your legs
    And some gelatin treat for your St. Vitus feet
    If I want to. If I want to.

(she continues singing these two verses)

Robot: *(singing in a loud voice)*
    One little, two little, three little witches
    Flying over rooftops, Flying over ditches,
    Four little, five little, six little
    witches.
    All on Halloween night.

The **Robot** *sticks his tongue out at the witch, and they seem about to have a fight when the* **Gypsy** *intervenes.*

Gypsy:
    I'm tired of all those games
    we've been playing.
    I want to tell ghost stories.

The group responds with enthusiasm for this suggestion.

Pirate: *(skeptical)*
>Do you really think we ought to?

Witch: *(belligerently)*
>Why not?

Robot:
>Because don't you remember what happened the last
>time?
>Nyah, nyah, nyah!
>That's when you got turned into a wicked witch!
>Ha! Ha! Ha!

*The **Witch** is ready to pounce on him, but the **Gypsy** holds
her back and the **Pirate** takes up the suggestion.*

Pirate:
>We all remember the nightmares.
>None of us slept well for days.

Witch: *(stomping her foot)*
>But it wasn't our fault.
>It was his! (she points to **Death** who has edged into the
>fringe area of the lighted part of the stage.)

*The children squeal with delight and run to drag **Death** into
the center of the spotlight. He kneels down on one knee and
they spread out around him on the floor.*

Gypsy:
>You shouldn't have shown us what you did.

Robot:
>Or who you are for that matter.

Gypsy:
>Or what business you had hanging around
>always on our fringes.

Pirate:
>You were nicer when you were the Magician.

Robot:
>Or the doctor in the sickroom.

Witch:
>You were even nicer as the shadow
>bleeding behind our parents.

Gypsy: *(gushing)*
> But now we love you!
> We see you as you are and
> things are better.
> You are as much a mystery at one end as
> our births are at the other.
> We know so little about you, except
> you cannot talk.

Death *nods and smiles.*
Robot:
> Seeing you in this light, it's
> hard to believe you were a thing we were
> taught to hate.

Gypsy:
> And run from in disgust.

Pirate:
> And never, never mention at the table.

They all laugh.
Gypsy:
> And to think that what we were taught to fear
> is only the embodiment of our constant companion.
> The shade to rest us from the heat and
> turmoil of our pleasure.

Robot:
> And all we ever needed to know and all we
> have to keep in mind until the end is that
> you haven't called us yet.

Pirate:
> In fact you will ask us for nothing,
> not even in that final act; no trading costumes
> or masks, no wasting a lifetime dreading one singular
> intrusion. You are here and have been with us since
> the incredible moment of our births.

Witch:
> And all the time what we really feared was starting
> each new day with old illusions. It really wasn't
> fair to hate the blank of some negative existence when
> the fact of the matter is we can't be cheated!

Gypsy:
> Yes, if we had viewed life as you do,
> we'd have seen the graceful curves and
> continuous flow, the delicate creases giving
> everything perspective.

Robot:
> And time is the only thing which can't be
> taught or learned.

Pirate:
> Or bought and sold.

Witch:
> Or traded with someone else.

Gypsy:
> Memories are only monuments and
> all our pale reflections are glass.
> We see the world through them.

Robot:
> Time is the one respect with which
> all men were not created equal.

Pirate:
> And yet it comes to each of us in equal pieces:
> one day at a time.

Witch:
> One moment!

Gypsy:
> Each second.

The **Male** *and* **Female** *enter carrying trays and party
favors, but they drop everything in horror at what they see*

Female:
> Monster! Bastard! Beast!
> *(she runs forward, grabbing the children and trying to
> shelter them from the sight and presence of* **Death***)*
> What are you doing here? Haven't you done enough
> Haven't you harmed them enough, done enough
> damage?

Isn't it enough we know your evil schemes and wicked
  plotting?
You steal us blind at every turn and leave us
stranded in suffering. You have a whore's body full
of gall. And as if that weren't havoc enough, do you have
to terrorize these children?

Male: *(charging forward and wrestling with* **Death***)*
  I'll tear you apart with my bare hands, you god-damned
  son of a bitch!

Male:
The **Male** *strong-arms* **Death** *who offers no resistance. As
he turns the body toward the* **Female,** *pinning* **Death's**
arms behind him, she winces in recognition.

Female:
  Oh no! Not you. Not here. Now.
  Those rank eyes and damp sockets.
  Those ugly teeth beneath that
  utter lack of hair. I'd know you anywhere.

  You reek with the odor of pungent breath
  and the solid smell of anesthesia that
  poisons my memory with its teeth.
  Strange cries.

  First my own and then others.
  Screams filtering down the wash of night
  bringing me sleep. And you standing in the
  shadows wherever children are born.

  How can you! You hell-monger, Death!

The **Female** *rushes to help her mate and together they drag
a limp and unprotesting* **Death** *off-stage.*

*After a few moments of silence, the children form a circle in
the center of the narrowed spotlight and begin to walk slowly
around; they begin singing softly:*

Here we go round the mulberry bush,
the mulberry bush, the mulberry bush;
Here we go round the mulberry bush,
so early in the morning, so early in the morning.

Here we go round the mulberry bush,
the mulberry bush, the mulberry bush;
Here we go round the mulberry bush,
as if it were a tree, as if it were a tree.

The **Chorus** *joins in singing this last stanza (forming
another circle around the children, turning the opposite
direction):*
This is the way the world will end,
the world will end, the world will end;
This is the way the world will end,
Not with a bang, but a
Spoken by all: *(softly, but distinctly)*
Whim-per!

*Immediately the stage goes dark and simultaneously one of
the girls states in a loud, exuberant voice!*

It smells like Easter!

Fine/The End